Praise From
The Heart

By
JULIE RAHLFS

www.xulonpress.com

Presented to

_____

As a Gift

_____

From

_____

Date

_____

SPECIAL THANKS

With a grateful heart I want to thank my long-time friend, Norma Ralls, for her encouragement, opinions and her unending patience. She has truly been an inspiration.

INTRODUCTION

Spending time with God, spending time in His word, speaking the word, praying, praise and worship, these are all keys to fellowshipping with Him. Believing the word of God in faith, praising Him from a grateful heart creates an unbeatable combination that is powerful in our daily lives. We will receive more benefits through a full understanding of God's love for us and His desire to fellowship with us. He wants to reveal His love for each one of us and immerse us in His love. Through our praise and worship, through our prayer and fellowship God will be there in the midst. So many of us think of praise and worship only in church, we miss the daily portion of praise and worship which is so vital

in our walk with our Lord.

It is my hope that you will find this teaching inspirational and move on into your own personal praise and worship lifting up the living, loving Holy Father God.

Praise from the heart, thanking Him for what He has promised in His word, faith He will accomplish what He has promised.

Give God praise continually even in the midst of a problem, before we see the victory, before there is a solution, He is there behind the scenes making a way, solving the problem, before you see HIS delivering power

"Let everything that has breath and every breath of life praise the Lord! Praise You the Lord! Psalms 150:6 Amp

PREFACE

Before entering in to praise each one of us should have accepted Jesus as Lord of their lives, believing Jesus is the son of God.

Ask for forgiveness for sins committed and forgive all who may have hurt you.

PRAYER OF SALVATION

I pray that you Lord will come into my heart and forgive me for all my sins and transgressions, I repent for going my own way in life. I believe you are the son of God as the Bible says you are and that you died in my place for my sins and rose again to give me life. I confess Jesus as my Lord and I ask for Him to come into my life and live in my heart. Give my life purpose and meaning.
In the Name of Jesus I pray   Amen

CONTENTS

WHY PRAISE

You manifest the Glory of God through praise and worship. God has chosen Worship to be an avenue through which He inhabits His people, those who are upright and in right standing with Him. Those who are in fellowship with him will praise and worship Him in Spirit and in truth from the heart. His presence dwells in the worship of those who love Him.

It takes faith to enter into a pure worship. This is where the power lies in the praise; the worship from deep within each individual, a heart adoring and honoring their Lord. It is this manifestation of worship that power from on high moves to meet the needs of the people of God. It takes faith to enter into a pure worship. Without faith it is impossible to please God. So in order to please God we must enter into praise with faith.

Expressing our love for Him is essential. God desires that we praise and worship him from the heart. He is worthy of our praise, He alone is worthy. He sacrificed his sinless life for us so that we could have life abundantly. If you want an abundant life, praise from the heart is essential.

God desires that we have no other gods before Him. No other gods like pride, false religions, idols of any kind, love of money, lofty ideas, work, materialism or anything that separates you from God the Father, anything that stands between you and God. How can anyone praise, from the heart, when God the Father is not first place in his life. Anything that we put ahead of God separates us from Him.

There are many who miss out on God's blessings because they refuse to praise and worship Him in their lives fellowshipping; they refuse to spend enough time with Him. This is a choice we have, to praise Him or not to praise Him. How much time have you given to praise God this month, this week, this day?

Do you praise only in church and then forget the rest of the week. Are you expressing a grateful heart for what God has done for you, His protection, His healing, His prosperity, watching over your family, are you grateful? Do you tell Him you are grateful daily?

When you love the Lord you will have the desire to praise Him, however not many believers do on a regular basis or at all. This is unfortunate, they miss out on most of what God truly has planned for them. Many don't realize just how important praise is for their walk with Him.

Praise is essential, but not for God, He doesn't have a need to be praised. However, we have a need and a desire to praise and exult Him. This attitude of praise causes us to keep a proper perspective of who we are and who He is and what He has done for us. However, I am sure He enjoys the praise and worship of His children, it gives Him pleasure.

The works of God are truly great and they are manifested in your life when you are willing to praise and glorify Him with a grateful heart.

He wants to bless you. He wants to give you the desires of your heart.

He wants you to enjoy an abundant life. Stop and praise Him often during the day. Take time for God throughout the day, praise Him in the car, take time at work, when at home give Him glory for what He does for you during the day.

There may be times when situations and circumstances in life can look impossible to you. However, standing firm and looking to the immovable word of God, believing Him to be there to fight the battle for you and He will when we learn to praise Him moment by moment even when we don't see any immediate results. God says He will take care of you when you trust in Him. No power of the enemy can come against you when you learn to praise God and stand on His word through faith.

Faith in God. Faith in His word. Faith in His ability. Faith that He loves you. Faith that He will do it for you. Praise and worship brings belief in all that God has for you.

HOW YOU ENTER INTO PRAISE

Praise requires action, something we do, a decision we make that turns into emotion. You having a grateful heart toward the Lord is essential to praise. You can praise the Lord with a grateful heart no matter where you find yourself in life.

If you find yourself having trouble, sickness, lack of any kind, give a sacrificial time of praise, you won't feel like it and it is not easy but you can do it and you must do it if you are going to move through any unpleasant situation with victory. You must praise your Father God so He can move you through the situation.

To praise God, start thanking Him for all that He has done for you and your family. Thank Him that your name is written in heaven. Thank Him for who He is, how wonderful He is. When giving thanks, you open the door that ushers you into the praise arena. Your relationship with Him is enhanced.

Music can help you break down the barriers that hinder you from entering into praise. The right kind of music can fill the heart and move the emotions to feel gratefulness toward God. That gratefulness will move you into a praise attitude.

Raise your hands in surrender, yes, raise all the way up as a child would do when wanting to be picked up, raise your hands to heaven and give God praise from your heart. Try it and see where it leads you, just begin to thank Him and then praise Him, give Him glory, give Him honor, give Him your heart, give Him your very self. God loves you and wants you to live a victorious life.

He wants to give you the desires of your heart. He wants to give you life abundantly; all that you need or ever will need in this life is yours through prayer, obedience, faith, praise and worship.

So many of us only praise in church when the music plays and we are encouraged to praise but the word implies, we are to praise Him all the time. "His praise will continually be in my mouth." But life gets in the way and praise is not constantly in our mouths, that is why this little book is being written and it is my hope that you will carry it with you wherever you go and look in it to find the words to begin your praise of God our Father.

FROM PRAISE TO WORSHIP

It's important to note that worship is not possible without praise. They, praise and worship, go together one then the other. Once you enter into praise don't stop, keep moving into the Lord, lean into him and you will soon be into worship. Worship is a deeper experience with God the Father. Move into it deeply, close your eyes and continue in worship, allow the tears to flow, allow yourself to just fill up with His presence, fill to over flowing. A warm glow of love will overcome you, a feeling of contentment and peace.

God inhabits the praise of His children. Just think, God is there with you in your private room, He is there finding pleasure in you as He hears your worship and He is working out your problems, healing your body and providing your needs. He gives you the desire of your heart just because you in love humbled yourself, bowed down and praised and worshiped Him, giving Him glory for all that He is and has done. Does it not please you and give you pleasure when your children give you praise and tell you what a wonderful father or mother you are. It makes you want to do whatever it is that they want, God is even more that way. He loves us with a love that we are unable to comprehend, experience or understand. Yet, we with the love that we know give to our children what they need or want how much more God the Father will give to us what we need or want when we walk in faith with a grateful heart with praise and worship for Him.

It doesn't matter what problems you have, God knows and He knows what to do to eliminate them, after all, He is your Savior, your Miracle worker, your Healer, your loving Father God. When we praise our Father, giving up our thoughts, giving Him our hearts, our all and all, this type of praise will turn into worship. Praising each day will give you the foundation to be able to move more freely into worship.

Thank you Father, give Him praise, glory and thanksgiving from the heart. Take communion frequently and thank Him for all that He has done. When taking communion deeply remember Jesus took it all on His body to free you, to redeem you, to heal you, to give you His righteousness, He bore it all so you would not have to bear anything, not anything! Cast all your care over on

Him for He cares for you. The mind will try to care but you don't pay attention, don't let the mind stray, stay focused on HIM.

BASKING IN HIS PRESENCE

You don't have to be on your knees or in a dark room or by yourself, there is no special place or time to praise and give worship to the Lord, He is always there and listening. Praise will bubble up from inside you and fill you with His person.

There will be times when breaking into praise is spontaneous and without thinking, "I am going to praise the Lord" praise will come to your mind and tears fill your eyes as you begin to just think on Him. This can be any place, any where and at any time.

As you begin to concentrate on the Lord and His Presence allow yourself to think only on Him and block out all else that would take your mind from who He is and what He has done for you. Close your eyes think on Him let Him consume you allow Him to fill you with Himself then think of Him and speak out the words that come to your mind. Take the time and bask in His presence, some tears will come to the eyes and a warm loving feeling will overcome you.

Basking in His presence is just allowing Him to surround you, there is nothing else to think, you are alone with Him and there is nothing else, there is just you and Him intertwined together in His love. You can stay in His presence for hours and think it has been only minutes; there is no time with the Lord. Stay with Him as long as you can to enjoy His presence. Let Him wrap His loving arms around you, to hold you in His presence.

Open your mind to Him with a grateful

heart and begin to give Him praise, worship and glory. In the next pages there are praise and worship examples for you to start with and as you begin let your heart enter into praise and it will lead you into worship and as you worship stay in that place and move on into the His presence. Don't allow yourself to get nervous or self-conscious, don't allow yourself to think on anything but Him, how wonderful He is... just enjoy Him and wait on Him, He will surround you in His love. He will pull you close. Wait on Him, listen within yourself and be quite, listen, wait and enjoy Him.

As you praise and worship the Lord you will want to write your own for the needs that you have in your life.

When you are ready to write your own praise and worship there are pages provided in the back of this book for your personal reference.

Begin to
PRAISE and WORSHIP

Open your mind, your heart and begin to give Him praise and glory

To my God in whom I trust, I praise and I honor You... You are my refuge... my fortress... my high tower... my everything... You are my provider... my healer... my friend in whom I trust... You are my all in all... there is none other than You my Lord... Praise is consistently in my heart and on my lips for there is none other like You my Lord... my life belongs to You and only You... You make me to dwell in safety and contentment... You watch over me carefully... loving me tenderly and thoroughly... In You I find myself... in You I am blessed... in You I have all I need... There is no need in You Father... I am complete in You... my very life is in You... glory to Your Name... I trust in You completely for You are my all in all... there is no other that can compare, O Lord my God, in You I trust... Prince of my peace... You are faithful... You will never leave me... My God my Savior... I open my heart to You O Lord... You are my all and all... Your kindness, Your mercy causes me to be grateful... Your love will last forever... Your mercy will last forever... Your word will last forever... Every heart beat I have is for You... You are my heart's desire... I pant after You Lord, my God... I hunger for all of You... I give my heart to You Lord... Be glorified... I give You honor and praise... Be glorified in all the earth... in the beauty of the mountains... the loveliness of the valleys... the flowers of bright colors... and the variety of animals... be gloried in all things my Lord...

Magnificent Lord... Magnificent Creator of the whole earth... I lift my eyes to You... my hands reach for You... You are worthy... so worthy to be praised and worshiped... Here I am I give You my heart... God of my life... Love of my life... I offer myself to You... You are always with me... I trust You in all... My hope is in You... King of my life... Prince of my peace... You are faithful... You will never leave me...You will never forsake me...

My God my Savior... I open my heart to You O Lord... You are my all and all... Your love will last forever... Your mercy will last forever... Your word will last forever... Every heart beat I have is for You my Savior... I call upon your name Jesus... Jesus... Jesus... Only You are the Savior of my spirit... Adoni... Elshadi my God... my Savior... my only Lord... You are so good to me... I call upon You Lord for all my needs... I humbly plea, take me Lord to Your special place of peace... into Your presence... let me bask in Your presence...

Let Your love and grace be upon me and move through me... Save me Lord... save me to Yourself... You have the power Jesus... that wonderful name of Jesus... freedom and hope to all is in the name of Jesus... You are above all... Your name is above all names... I exalt You... Higher, higher take me with You Lord... higher and higher... You can do anything when I call on Your name, Jesus... Jesus precious name of Jesus...

I want to worship You for who You are... my Lord... my Savior... my King... Beautiful Savior... You are so beautiful to me... Oh Lord you are my only Lord and you are beautiful to me.... Only You are Holy... Holy, Holy are You Lord... Holy, Holy are You Lord... Holy are You Lord...

All creation will sing Holy, Holy to the King of Kings, the Lord of Lords... You are an amazing God, my Father... Amazing in all that You do... and have done... amazing for who You are I praise You most Holy One for only You are faithful... faithful to guide me... faithful to teach me in Your wisdom... in Your ways... Praise be to You Father God... my Abba Father... I honor you... I love You, I give You my life, my very being lives in You... Great is the Lord... greatly to be praised...

You are my life... You make my life worth living... My heart takes courage in You Lord... I take courage and stand strong in You my Lord... I hope in You Lord... in all Your Greatness... in Your Majesty... Take me lord... take all of me... You are my life Lord... I am longing for the day to be with You always...

I give You thanks for Your righteousness... I give thanks to You Lord for all You do for me and my family...those I love and care for... I give thanks to You Lord for Your grace... I will praise your name... I will lift my voice to You Lord... I rejoice in You... I lift up my hands to You... I crawl into Your arms... You hold me with deep love... You caress me with Your love... You hold me in Your arms... There is no other like You... I give You glory due Your name... I worship You Lord in beauty and holiness...

I praise You for Your goodness... Your wisdom... Your love... Your kindness... I worship You Lord for all You are... Praise be to You Father for all spiritual blessings You have given unto me... Thank you Father for You are the almighty and powerful God of my life... Abba Father... Abba Father...

Thank You for Your peace... Your mercy... Bring me close to You Father... draw me near unto You... enlighten my understanding with Your wisdom... let Your ways fill me totally... let Your love overflow from me to others... only Your love is perfect... May I always lift You up and glorify Your name... Guide me in Your truth and faithfulness... Show me Your ways my Lord... teach me Your paths... Oh my God, I trust in You... I am confident in You...

My hope is in You only and only in You... Your goodness surrounds me... You O Lord lead me with sweet love... Oh how I love You Lord... just Love You with all my being... with all that is within me... There is no other like you my Lord..., my Savior... There is no other like You... All the paths of the Lord are mercy and steadfast love...

You who is faithful and unwavering in His love for me... You who forgives me of all my iniquities... You who washes me clean and makes me white as snow... You who pardons my quilt... You who cares for me more than I know... I give You all my love and adoration... I reverently fear and worship the Lord who is great... Thank you Holy Spirit for the guidance and power to stay clean and pure before You... beautiful before the Lord praising Him all the day long...

Fill me with Your love Lord... I sing praises unto You my Lord... praises and glory be Yours and Yours alone... I rejoice in You O Lord for You are gracious to me... I rejoice in your wisdom... in the understanding that You give unto me from your word...

I praise and worship Your majesty... You O Lord are faithful... only You are faithful... You most Holy One are faithful... faithful to guide... faithful to teach me in Your wisdom... faithful to bring me to Your word and reveal to me Your mighty ways... Teach me Your will for my life... praise be to You Father God...

Thank You Father for Your deliverance from the evil one who attempts to kill, steal and destroy all that You have so graciously given... I rejoice in the victory You have set before me... I constantly renew my mind in the spirit having a fresh mental and spiritual attitude... putting on the new nature of Jesus... Great is the Lord... and greatly is He to be praised... He has given unto me so I give unto others freely from my heart... I give because that is Your way Lord... when I give of anything You most gracious Father gives back unto me... Praise be to You Father of Glory... how I thank you and glorify Your name... bring my spirit into oneness with Your Spirit... letting all pollution and evil speaking be far from me... let it never come out of my mouth... only praise... only worship... only blessings... giving grace to those who hear it... praise be to You Father of Glory... how I thank You Lord of all... I glorify Your name...

Thank you Father that I am sealed

with the precious Holy Spirit... branded as God's own... secured for the day of redemption... praise to Jesus for victory... Let me become useful, Lord... helpful and kind to others... tender-hearted with compassion and under-standing... loving as You love... Your loving kindness is before my eyes... I love the place where Your glory dwells...

My eyes are ever toward the Lord... looking for Him... seeing Him in every-thing... The Lord is my salvation... He is my light... The Lord is my refuge... my stronghold... He is my life... my all in all...

In Him will I be confident... my heart will not fear... who is greater than the Lord... You O Lord are my protec-tion... my hiding place... You cover me with your pinions... your feathers... I am protected in You... only You Lord

God... For in the day of trouble You hide me in Your secret place... You hide me in Your shelter... I will not let my heart be troubled... I will be strong and will take courage in all You are... I will hope and wait for You... I expect You Lord... You are my rock... my fortress... my refuge... I give You glory... glory... I give You honor and glory... I love to worship You... Holy... Holy... You are... God Almighty full of glory... I love to worship You... to come before You gratefully... Holy is the Lord... I love You Lord... my God Almighty... Holy is my Lord... who I love... I love to worship You my Lord.... You give me beauty for ashes... You give me peace... joy... happiness... You give me strength... wholeness... You give me all I need... I will glory in You Lord... You hold my future... I will hold on to You Lord forever... You are Worthy... You are Holy... You are faithful... I lift up my hands unto Lord... I cry Holy... Holy is the Lord... You are My Savior... My heart is Yours Lord... I bow down before You in worship...

Thank You for Your grace... for Your mercy... Jesus... Jesus... be blessed... blessed is thy name... I don't ever want to be without You... You are my life... Lead me Lord in Your wonderful ways... teach me... I will hear Your voice... I will hear Your sweet voice... I love You Lord with all my heart...I will follow You to the end.... What can I do for You Lord... Let me be of use to You Lord... Let my life count for You Lord... Let me bask in Your presence... Not to ever leave You... Let Your kingdom live in me... live through me fully... Lead me Lord in Your ways... As You are so I am... Show me the wonders of Your love...

Gracious Father I praise You for all

that You have done... are doing and will do in my life... Thank You Father for Your great and mighty ways... I love You Lord... only You can draw me near to You... You bring spiritual blessings to me... You fill me with goodness and loving kindness... only You Lord and no other is worthy of my praise... Through You I am free... delivered... forgiven... loved and saved... Beautiful are You Lord... I love You Lord... worship You and You alone... my Father God...

I praise You Lord... Praise you most Holy One... The Lord is my rock... my fortress... my deliverer... my God in whom I take refuge... blessed be the name... blessed be the mighty one...

My Lord of heaven and earth... the everlasting one... Praise You Father for all that You have done for me...

Blessed be the Lord... He has heard

my cry... The Lord is my strength... He is my shield... My heart trusts and relies on Him... I give Him glory... I sing glory... glory unto Him... I am confident in Him... lean on Him... He is my strength... He is my stronghold... my salvation... I give him all my praise and rejoice in Him... I sing unto the Lord with my whole heart... I give You gratitude from my heart... In Your favor is life... I am grateful...

I will be glad and rejoice in His mercy... in His Love for me... I give thanks to You... I rejoice in Your marvelous ways... I sing praises to Your beautiful Name... I give thanks and am greatful for the mercy... for the loving kindness the Lord shines on me and my family... You are wonderful in Your majesty... beautiful in Your holiness... so pure are You ... You are all I want... all I live for... You are my life... You are my treasure...

You are glorious... I worship You Lord... I sing to You with high praise... You will never leave me... You will always be near to me... Lord You are my love... my life... my very being... there is no other so worthy... You have so blessed me... I am grateful for all that You have given to me... You are all I need... You are the only one that I need... the only one... it's Your love that gives me strength...

I shall be joyful in the Lord... I shall rejoice in His deliverance for He is great and greatly to be praised... God of all creation... I give You praise... Praise to the great I AM, full of power and might...

Thank You Lord for Your love... Your caring ways fill me... Thank you for Your grace... Thank You for forgiveness... Your Mercy endures forever... Thank

You for the healing You have provided... Thank You for all You are... for all You have made me, Thank You Lord... You are my all in all... there is no other like You... Higher, higher, take me with You Lord higher and higher You can do anything when I call on Your name Jesus, Jesus precious name of Jesus I want to worship You for who You are, my Lord Savior, my King and beautiful, beautiful to me... O Lord You are my only Lord and beautiful to me... Only You Holy... Holy, Holy are You Lord... Holy, Holy are you Lord... Holy are You Lord...

All creation will sing Holy, Holy to the King of Kings, the Lord Jesus... Great is the Lord greatly to be praised are You Lord...

You are an amazing God, my Father amazing in all that You do.... I praise

You most Holy One for only You are faithful, faithful to guide me and teach me in Your wisdom... Praise be to You Father God...

Gracious Father I praise You for all that You have done... all that You are doing and will do in my life.... Thank You Father for Your great and mighty ways...

I love You Lord, only You can draw me near to You, You bring spiritual blessing to me... You fill me with goodness and loving kindness only You Lord and no other is worthy of my praise... Through You I am free, delivered, forgiven, loved and saved... Beautiful are You Lord, I love You Lord and worship You Father... Praise You Lord, Praise You most Holy One...The Lord is my rock and my fortress and my deliverer my God in whom I take refuge blessed be Your name, blessed be the mighty One, the Lord of heaven and earth, the everlasting One...

Praise You Father for all that You have done for me, I praise You for Your goodness, Your wisdom, Your love, Your kindness praise be to You Father for all spiritual blessings and that You have given unto me. Thank You Father for You are the almighty and powerful God of my life... Abba Father... Glory to the Lord who is awesome... Awesome is the Lord... In Your presence there is peace... love... I will praise You for all eternity... hallelujah... hallelujah... Hallelujah... Praise to the Father, Son and Holy Spirit... Be glorified... be glorified my Lord... I lift You up and praise Your name forever...

Guide me... move me... wherever You

need me lead me... show me... fill me... use me... Let the glory of the Lord rise up in me... You are all I need... all I want is You... My God is my exceeding joy... I will always praise Him... He is my healer... He is my healer... There is healing in Him... in Him alone... I exult You Lord... I lift You up on high... I Glorify You...

Your majesty is everywhere... in the mountains... in the sea... in the sky... in the deserts... in the night... in the day... in the flowers... colors... trees... plants... Your majesty is awesome... How great is my God... How wonderful is my God... my Father... He is wonderful in every way... I belong to You... I will always be Yours... How wonderful... how marvelous is my Savior... I take pleasure in worshiping You... singing praises to my Lord... There is nothing that compares with You my Lord... You are my all in all.... my everything... How mighty... how worthy are You Lord... I come into Your presence Lord to love You... to be with you... to spend time with You... I Give You glory and Praise... Worshiping You... Hallaulua... You reign... Holy... Holy... worthy is the Lamb... Worthy are You Lord...blessed is the Lord... how You refresh me Lord...

Lord God Almighty... Holy... You alone are worthy Lord... Father God I lift You up... Lift up Your name... I trust in You Jesus... I depend on You Lord... I worship You Lord... Holy are You Lord... I love You... my almighty one... You alone are my hearts desire... I love to praise You Lord... I love to be close to You... to be in Your arms...to climb into Your Lap... to have you hold me... there is none like You... I give You praise for all that You have given me... there is none like You... I praise You for my health... I praise You for my family... I give thanks unto the Lord of Lords... Your mercy is everlasting... it's new every morning... You alone do great wonders... Your mercy endures forever... I give thanks for You are the one who delivers me from my enemies... Your mercy endures forever... I love You... I give thanks to my Father God whose mercy and loving kindness endures forever... Praise and glory to the God of gods... Only You are worthy of praise and only You are worthy of worship... Only You Lord and only You make my life new... Your mercy endures forever... Surround me with Your love...

I lift my voice and worship You my Lord for You are worthy to be praised... Only You deserve all my praise and worship... Only You deserve all the glory for You are worthy... I praise You for all the victories... the great victories... I praise you for all that You have done... all the great victories... for redeeming me from all of my troubles... for your mercy that endures forever... your forgiveness... Praise You for who You are my Father... Honor and glory are Yours my Lord... I give to the Lord honor and praise... I lift you up Lord... Let the Lord be magnified... magnified forever I worship You in beauty and holiness...

Thank You for your peace... Your mercy... bring me close to You Father... draw me near unto You... enlighten my understanding with Your wisdom... let Your ways fill me totally... let Your love overflow from me to others... only Your love is perfect...

May I always lift You up... I glorify Your name... thank You Holy Spirit for the guidance...for power to stay clean... to be beautiful before the Lord... praising him all the day long. Fill me with Your love Lord... I sing praises unto You my Lord... praises and glory be Yours... I rejoice in You O Lord... rejoice in Your wisdom... in the understanding that You give unto me of Your word...

I praise and worship your majesty O Lord... You are faithful... You most holy one are faithful... faithful to guide... to teach Your wisdom... faithful to bring me to Your word... revealing to me Your mighty ways... Your will for my life... praise be to You Father God.

Thank you Lord that I dwell in the secret place of the Most High God... I abide in the shadow of the almighty...

Thank You Lord that by Your stripes I am healed from the top of my head to bottom of my feet.... My body is healed totally.... My body is healed totally... every organ... every muscle... every artery functions perfectly... my body is whole and complete... My heart is not troubled... my eyes are not dim... my body is whole... functioning perfectly.... I don't go by sight or by what I feel but by the Word of God that is the only real truth... I am the healed one because of what You have done for me...

Thank You Lord for your favor that surrounds me.... Your wonderful Favor that goes before me... follows behind me... Let the favor and delightfulness that is Yours Lord be upon me... thank You for establishing the works of my hands for Your good...

Thank You Lord for the armor that You have given to me, I put it on everyday...Thank You for the helmet of salvation... the breastplate of righteousness, for I am the righteousness of God in Christ Jesus... I put on the shoes of the gospel of peace... I take up the shield of faith to fight off the wiles of the devil and the sword of the spirit to rightly divide the word of God... thank You Lord... You have provided it all...

You and You alone are my refuge my fortress... I trust in You... I know that I can rely on You to care for me.... Thank you Father that I have no fear because You are there... Your shield and faithfulness are a buckler for me...

Thank You that I have health... I will not fear... I will not be afraid of the pestilence that stalks in darkness or of the destruction that lays waste in the day... thank you Father that You have given Your angles charge over me, to accompany me... defend me in all my ways... Thank You Lord... I am grateful... so very grateful...

It is good and wonderful to give thanks unto You Lord and sing praises to Your name... I give You thanks Father God... I give You glory... I give You honor... to You only... I am planted in the house of the Lord... I will flourish in the courts of my God... in Him only do I live and find my life...

Thank You Father, You are my deliverer... my refuge... You are the one I run to... I hide in Your special place... Thank you my Lord for all that You are and that You have done and are going to do... I love You so much...You are my peace... my contentment... my wholeness is in You... I find rest... I am not afraid... Your presence is with me always...

Thank You for carrying me through troubled times for You care for me... You deliver me from all trouble... I trust in You only... You O Lord are by protector, my defender in You I am safe... hidden in Your arms of love... I surrender to Your love... Thank You my Lord that You are there, You are my everything and all in all I adore You and You alone... You are my all in all I adore You

I lift your name I lift it up on high there is no other name like your name Jesus, Jesus, Almighty one...Your name is wonderful and wonderful are You Lord...

You are my strength... I come to You with joy in my heart, for You are my joy... come wrap Your loving arms around me and hold me close let me not fall away... Love me Lord as I give my heart to You...hear my heart cry Lord as I love You with all my being... Come hold my heart, come inhabit my worship, nothing is as wonderful to me as spending time with You... Let Your amazing love infill me... take me deeper Lord into You... I want to know You more... Holy Spirit lead me into more...

Praise... Honor... Glory be Yours... only Yours my Lord... my Savior... Yahweh, my only God, my Father...

WRITE YOUR PRAISE AND WORSHIP

Thank you Lord from a grateful heart for...

_____

_____

_____

_____

_____

_____

_____

_____

_____

_____

_____

_____

_____

_____

WRITE YOUR PRAISE AND
WORSHIP FROM YOUR HEART.....

_____

_____

_____

_____

_____

_____

_____

_____

_____

_____

_____

_____

_____

_____

_____

_____

_____

_____

_____

WRITE YOUR PRAISE AND WORSHIP HERE

_____

_____

_____

_____

_____

_____

_____

_____

_____

_____

_____

_____

_____

_____

_____

_____

_____

_____

CPSIA information can be obtained at www.ICGtesting.com
Printed in the USA
BVOW07s1942200114

342487BV00001B/8/P